Prayers for the Promise

Prayers for the Promise
by Kristi Woods

ISBN-13: 978-1732448681

Copyright © 2019 Kristi Woods

Edited by LeeAnn Knowles

Commissioned by The King's Company
Odessa, Texas

Published by Lazarus Tribe Media
Rome, Georgia

Printed in the United States of America.

www.thekingscompany-creations.com
www.lazarustribemedia.com

Prayers for the Promise

by Kristi Woods

THE KING'S COMPANY
ODESSA, TEXAS

Lazarus Tribe Media
Rome, Georgia

Foreword

Dearest Friend,

Thank you for reaching out and picking up this book. My prayer for you is that you will do more than simply skim through it or rush the reading in between tasks. Take some time, sit down in the quiet, and let the words from these verses soak into your heart as your prayers cry out to your Abba Daddy. Because you see, praying for the promise isn't just about getting what you want. It's about growing closer to the One who loves you enough to give you the gift in the first place. That's where peace is. That's where power is found. In His presence. May we all be found more and more at the feet of Jesus.

-Kristi

1

Zechariah 8:6

This is what the Lord of Heaven's Armies says, All this may seem impossible to you now, a small remnant of God's people. But is it impossible for me?

Lord,

I confess that there is a lot about my situation that seems very impossible to me. It is easy for me to be overwhelmed with all the "No's." The medical reports, the test results, the re-occurring proof that my miracle has not come yet. But you remind me when my vision is clouded by doubt that you, the Lord of Heaven's Armies, are a big God. You are bigger than all the negativity in my life. You are so mighty and powerful; my human brain can scarcely take it in. Nothing, not one single thing, is impossible for you. You do not need encouraging medical reports or test results to bring forth a miracle. You are God, there is none like you.

Thank you for being the God of the impossible!

2

1 Samuel 1:10-11, 19b-20

Hannah was in deep anguish, crying bitterly as she prayed to the Lord. And she made this vow, "O Lord of Heaven's Armies if you will look upon my sorrow and answer my prayer and give me a son, then I will give him back to you. He will be yours for his entire lifetime, and as a sign that he has been dedicated to the Lord, his hair will never be cut." When Elkanah slept with Hannah, the Lord remembered her plea, and in due time she gave birth to a son. She named him Samuel for she said, "I asked the Lord for him."

Lord,

I come to you with the humble heart of a servant. I am deep in anguish and weeping as I pray. Please look upon my sorrow and answer my prayer for a child in my womb. I know that you are good and sovereign; you are above time, help me to be patient as I wait. Comfort me and fill me with your peace. Encourage my heart and reassure me that a baby is coming.

Keep my focus on you, even when this long-awaited child is in my arms. Help me to release this child back to you; knowing that you love them more than I do. You have big plans for this little one. Give me a faithful heart like Hannah. I dedicate this child to you, Lord.

Thank you for remembering me!

3

Psalm 146:5-6

*But joyful are those who have the God of Israel as
their helper, whose hope is in the Lord their God.
He made heaven and earth, the sea, and everything
in them. He keeps every promise forever.*

Oh Lord, you are such a big God. You made everything without work or strain; but simply by your powerful spoken word. You have created so much; who am I that you would love me and desire a relationship with me? I fail you so often, and yet you still love me. You love me with a heart so big, that I struggle to comprehend it.

Remind me, Lord, when I get lost in the struggles and limitations of this world, that you are above them all! My joy is in you. You alone are my helper. You alone have the power and authority to work miracles in my life. My hope is forever in you, Lord.

Thank you for being a God who keeps every promise forever!

4

Hebrews 6:18-19

So God has given both his promise and his oath. These two things are unchangeable because it is impossible for God to lie. Therefore, we who have fled to him for refuge can have great confidence as we hold to the hope that lies before us. This hope is a strong and trustworthy anchor for our souls. It leads us through the curtain into God's inner sanctuary.

Lord,

Let me soak in your presence today. Thank you for being
a God who cannot lie. I praise you, for your promises and
oaths are unchangeable and true. I take refuge in your
character that overcomes my circumstances. You are a strong
and trustworthy anchor for my soul. Help me to hold tight to
you, when the seas of worry and grief come against me. Fill
me with your hope and bold confidence to trust your leading
in all things. Lead me into the sanctuary of your presence.
Cleanse my heart, draw me close to you, my refuge.

Thank you for your promises!

5

Isaiah 41:18-20

I will open up rivers for them on the high plateaus. I will give them fountains of water in the valleys. I will fill the desert with pools of water. Rivers fed by springs will flow across the parched ground. I will plant trees in the barren desert; cedar, acacia, myrtle, olive, cypress, fir, and pine. I am doing this so all who see this miracle will understand what it means; that it is the Lord who has done this, the Holy One of Israel who created it.

Lord,

Thank you for your provision and comfort. When I feel stuck on a high plateau, down in the valley, or lost in the desert; you fill me with the living water of your Holy Spirit. You refresh and renew me. Thank you, Lord!

Abba Daddy, bring life to my barren desert. Allow us to conceive our miracle baby. Not just because this baby will bring us so much joy; but mostly to show the world who you are. You are always good and always faithful. You are alive, and you desire to bless those who earnestly seek you. Help us to seek you above all else. Flood us with your presence, Holy Spirit.

I worship you, Lord!

6

Job 10:10-12

*You guided my conception and formed me in the womb.
You clothed me with skin and flesh, and you knit my bones
and sinews together. You gave me life and showed me
your unfailing love. My life was preserved by your care.*

Abba Daddy,

You are the Creator. Not man, not science. Only you. Thank
you for creating me. Thank you for this life you have given
me. You are so good!

Lord, I pray this verse specially over the sweet baby you have
told us will come. Please guide our little one's conception.
Form them safely in my womb. Clothe them with skin and
flesh, healthy and without defect. Knit their bones and
sinews together with strength; preparing them for the call
you have placed on their life. You have shown me your love
in so many beautiful ways over the last few months. Bring
life to my barren places. Preserve our little miracle by your
good and faithful care.

Thank you, Lord!

7

Psalm 13:5-6

But I trust in your unfailing love. I will rejoice because you have rescued me. I will sing to the Lord because he is good to me.

Abba Daddy,

You alone are Lord over my life. Thank you for your love that never fails. Thank you for not making me earn your love, for I could never measure up. You have rescued me from a life of sin. You rescue me now from fear and loneliness. Even in my dark days, you pour out your grace and mercy on me.

I will sing to you, Lord, because you are good to me. When a door closes, help me to praise you in the hallway. May my praise, even in difficult times, be like the praises of Paul and Silas in prison. Use my praise to usher in breakthrough. Break through the evil schemes causing delay. Make me aware of, and help me to repent of, any unconfessed sin in my life that is separating me from the blessings you have prepared. Break through the heartache of this wait, and fill us with a peaceful calm instead. Let your glory shine through my life, as you give us our miracle baby.

All glory to you, God!

8

2 Thessalonians 3:3-5

But the Lord is faithful; he will strengthen you and guard you from the evil one. May the Lord lead your hearts into a full understanding and expression of the love of God and the patient endurance that comes from Christ.

Lord,

Waiting is hard. I grow weary when I can't see progress. I get impatient. Forgive me, Lord. I trust you. I know that you are always faithful. Keep me safe from evil that seeks to prey on my hurting heart. Breathe your life in me. Give me the strength to keep persevering in hope. Lead my heart to a full understanding of your love for me. Fill me with the patient endurance that comes only from you; allowing me to have peace and to fully trust you while I wait.

I praise you for your faithfulness!

9

Romans 4:18

Even when there was no reason for hope, Abraham kept hoping, believing that he would become the father of many nations. For God had said to him, "That's how many descendants you will have!"

Lord,

You know my heart. You know the pain and disappointment I am feeling. Come near to me, Abba Daddy. Remind me of the promise you gave of a baby. Refresh my spirit and renew my hope. Show me how to hope like Abraham did. I know it is more than just wishful thinking.

Help me to really believe that you will fulfill your promise. Cast out all fear and doubt, that I may have heard you wrong. Instead, fill me with your inexplicable peace. Give me a secure hope, a knowing, that you will do what you have said. Fill me with your grace as I wait. Keep me walking, closely with you, no matter what happens in my life.

Thank you, Lord! I love you!

10

Psalm 17:6

I am praying to you because I know you will answer,
O God. Bend down and listen as I pray.

Lord,

I come before you as your humble servant. I pray to you, for I know you will answer. Abba Daddy, bend down, be near to me, and listen as I pray. You gave me a promise that you were going to give us a biological child; a miracle baby. You said that you are not just doing this for us, but also to show others that you are real. You are the same today as you were in the Bible. You are all powerful and loving at the same time. You eagerly wait to bless those who believe and earnestly seek you. Help me to actively believe in our coming miracle, and to be intentional about earnestly seeking you above all else.

I love you, Lord!

11

Luke 1:45

*You are blessed because you believed that
the Lord will do what He said.*

Abba Daddy,

Thank you for being a God who cares enough about me, to promise me a miracle. I know that nothing is impossible for you. Help me to take that knowing from my head to my heart. I confess that I am scared. I am scared to get my hopes up. I am scared of disappointment and discouragement. I am scared that maybe I heard you wrong, maybe this is all just my own wishful thinking. But then you come. You cast out my fear and fill me with a peace that can only come from you. Jesus, you renew and solidify my faith. You give me hope and encouragement. You did give me a promise. When I choose to focus on you, not on my wait; I find that I can believe with confidence. I can rest in the security that you are always good and always faithful. Holy Spirit, fill me with faith and courage. I believe you God.

I believe you!

12

Amos 4:13

*For the Lord is the one who shaped the mountains,
stirs up the winds, and reveals his thoughts to
mankind. He turns the light of dawn into darkness
and treads on the heights of the earth. The
Lord God of Heaven's Armies is his name!*

Lord,

I look at this world you have created, and I can't help but to stand in awe of you. You made everything, not with hard labor or pain, but merely by your spoken word. Help me not to take you for granted!

Thank you, Abba Daddy, for revealing your thoughts to me. Who am I that you should care about me and yet, your love for me is so big and so full, that it is literally impossible for my meager mind to comprehend. Thank you for loving me! Thank you for revealing to me the promise of a child. When I start to doubt or overthink, drowning in my circumstances, remind me of how big you are. Speak this promised new little life into existence, and it will be done.

All glory to you, God!

13

Psalm 113:2-3, 5-7, 9

Blessed be the name of the Lord, now and forever. Everywhere-from the east to west - praise the name of the Lord. Who can be compared with the Lord our God who is enthroned on high? He stoops to look down on heaven and on earth. He lifts the poor from the garbage dump. He gives the childless woman a family, making her a happy mother. Praise the Lord!

Oh Lord,

You are so good! Even in heaven, surrounded by multitudes praising you; you love me enough to stoop and look down towards me. You see me struggling. You see me striving to push through, to be strong, to keep going. Daddy, you know my heart longs for a child. My arms ache to hold our precious newborn. Thank you for hearing me. Your compassion moves you to lift my heart out of the garbage dump. Lord, fill this woman's arms with a baby of her own. Fulfill this longing that refuses to be quenched. We believe you can do this Lord. You are our Mighty God. There is none like you!

Blessed be the name of the Lord, now and forever!

14

Genesis 21:1-2

The Lord kept his word and did for Sarah exactly what he had promised. She became pregnant, and she gave birth to a son for Abraham in his old age. This happened at just the time God had said it would.

Lord,

Thank you for this reminder that you do keep your promises. I know without a doubt that you have promised us a child. Lord, I lift our bodies up to you. Improve and repair our physical selves. Create an environment ready to grow our developing baby. Prepare our hearts to receive this answer to prayer. Give us grace, peace, and unity in our marriage as we wait. You are never too early, and you are never too late. Give us the courage to trust your timing, and never to give up hope. We know that you will do exactly what you promise, at just the time you said it would happen. Thank you for your faithfulness, Lord. Thank you for encouraging and sustaining us while we wait.

We love you, Lord!

15

Romans 15:4

Such things were written in the scriptures long ago to teach us. And the scriptures give us hope and encouragement as we wait patiently for God's promises to be fulfilled.

Abba Daddy,

Thank you for preserving your Word all these years. Thank you for revealing it to me today. Thank you for the peace, hope, love, impartation, and wisdom I receive through the scriptures. Help me to dig into your Word daily. Help me to seek you above all else. Cut away all the distractions, and keep my heart turned to you alone.

Lead me to the specific verse I need, at just the right time. Refill my hope and refresh my soul. Give me the peace to wait patiently for your promise to be fulfilled.

I treasure your Word!

16

Psalm 5:1-3

O Lord, hear me as I pray; pay attention to my groaning. Listen to my cry for help, my King and my God, for I pray to no one but you. Listen to my voice in the morning, Lord. Each morning I bring my requests to you and wait expectantly.

Abba Daddy,

Hear me as I pray. You feel my pain; you know my heartache.
Help me, Lord, my King, and my God. There is none like you.
My hope lies with you alone. You are the Exalted One; the
only one that can do what you have promised.

Listen to my voice, Daddy. Help me to make my time alone
with you each morning my number one priority. No one else
deserves my time like you do. Forgive me when I choose
selfishness over sacrifice. You always bless our time together.
Help me to crave more time in your presence.

I boldly come before your throne of grace; thank you for
hearing my requests. Thank you for never getting tired of me.
Give me the faith to wait in solid expectation. You WILL do
what you have said.

There will be miracles!

17

Micah 7:15

"Yes", says the Lord, "I will do mighty miracles for you, like those I did when I rescued you from slavery in Egypt."

Abba Daddy,

Thank you for giving me perspective while I wait. When I start to feel like I have been waiting too long, remind me that the Israelites waited in Egypt for hundreds of years, and yet, you did not forget them. You created a burning bush that was not consumed; you turned a staff into a serpent. You sent horrific plagues to change the heart of a cruel king, and you parted a sea; providing a dry escape route for your people.

When you promise to do a miracle in my life, I know it will happen. You have proven your magnificent power and faithfulness, time, and time again. Thank you for being the God that makes a way when there seems to be no way.

I love you, Lord!

18

Psalm 94:18-19

I cried out, "I am slipping!", but your unfailing love, O Lord, supported me. When doubts filled my mind, your comfort gave me renewed hope and cheer.

Abba Daddy,

I am trying. I am trying so hard to keep the faith. I am treading water in a sea of doubt, fighting to keep my chin up. I am slipping! But you O Lord, you are so good. Your big, powerful arm came down into the depths where I was. Your loving hand scooped me up and brushed me off. Holy Spirit, renew my mind. Remind me of the reasons behind my hope. Lord, reignite the joy inside of me that says; one day soon, I will be holding that which my heart cries out for now. Thank you for steadying me. Thank you for saving me when I begin to fall. You are so good. Thank you for coming to me when I need you!

I cry out to you, Abba Daddy!

19

Hebrews 10:23

Let us hold tightly without wavering to the hope we affirm, for God can be trusted to keep his promise.

Thank you, Lord, for this reminder today. Wrap your arms around me, help me to hold tightly without wavering. Sometimes, I give in to the weariness. I start to doubt, not in your holy power, but in my own understanding of you. I start to worry that I heard you wrong and am now putting myself through needless heartache.

But then you bring me a verse like today. You calm my heart and encourage my spirit. You reaffirm the promise you have made to me. You will always do what you have said you will do.

When I am scared to get my hopes up, when doubt begins to chip away at my heart, turn me to you; the giver of my hope. Fill me with your love and peace. Thank you for being a God I can trust to keep your promise.

I hold tightly to you, God!

20

Psalm 112:7

*They do not fear bad news; they confidently
trust the Lord to care for them.*

Oh Jesus,

You know my heart. You know my fears that tumble around in my mind. Jesus, help me to lay those fears down at your feet; and to stop picking them back up. My faith does not depend on what that test will show. My faith does not come from what the doctor says. My faith lies in you alone.

Right now, I am tossing out everything else that I have let get in my head. From now on, I only want to hear your voice. I will choose to trust you confidently, regardless of the news I get. Because you are my God, you love me, you care for me, and you only do what is best for me... at the best time. My heart and my mind are yours. Because of you, I do not fear bad news. You are my faithful God.

I trust you, Lord!

21

Psalm 6:8-9

The Lord has heard my weeping. The Lord has heard my plea; the Lord will answer my prayer.

Abba Daddy,

I know that you are full of compassion. I know that you have heard my weeping. When my heart is breaking, and I am sobbing, you are there. When I am angry shouting, "Why?" and "How much longer must I wait?," you are there. You let me feel all the feels. I can be real with you. No thought is hidden from you. I need your grace, Daddy. Please give me your supernatural grace to get through this. Flood me with your peace, Holy Spirit. Don't let me get bogged down with disappointment, doubt, and despair. Deliver me from these things, in Jesus' Name!

I know you have heard me, Lord. I climb into your gentle embrace as you warm my spirit with your peace. Give me rest and assurance that I did hear you right. At the exact time you have appointed, your glory will be revealed in my life. Our miracle will be here; our prayers WILL be answered!

Thank you, Daddy!

22

Psalm 145:13b-15

...The Lord always keeps his promises; he is gracious in all he does. The Lord helps the fallen and lifts those bent beneath their loads. The eyes of all look to you in hope, you give them their food as they need it.

Abba Daddy,

Thank you for being our Lord. Thank you for always keeping your promises. Thank you for your grace that comforts and consoles me like a personal hug from you. Help me, Lord. Lift my chin when my burdens weigh me down. Help me to shift my eyes and my focus on you. Thank you for your tender care. I praise you for being a faithful God I can trust; even when my situation seems dim. Flood me with your peace, love, and grace to keep waiting. Renew my strength and draw me closer to you, my only source of true hope.

You are my gracious God!

23

Psalm 145:5-6

I will meditate on your majestic glorious splendor and your wonderful miracles. Your awe-inspiring deeds will be on every tongue; I will proclaim your greatness.

Precious Lord,

Your Word is full of your wonderful miracles. People are healed, food is supernaturally multiplied, captives are freed, barren women are suddenly with child, and your precious Son has conquered death, allowing us to live freely in close relationship with you.

You inspire me to worship you with awe. Your goodness is so much greater, so much bigger, than any word I know to describe it. Use me, Lord. Let your glory be revealed in my life. Let others see your power by sending us our promised miracle baby. Help me never to miss a moment to give you all the praise and honor you deserve. When that precious little one is snuggled in my arms, I will praise you. Even now, as I kneel before your throne, I will praise you. Everyone will see your love and glory through your work in my life.

Thank you, Abba Daddy. All glory and honor to you; now and forever more!

24

Psalm 120:1

*I took my troubles to the Lord, I cried out
to Him, and He answered my prayer.*

Thank you, Lord for hearing my prayer. Thank you for holding close to your heart the silent whispers I lift up to you. I see other moms and their babies, and I look forward with the anticipation to the day when we get to meet our sweet babe. When I see other women lovingly pat their precious baby bumps, I find my hand resting on my waiting place. Help me to remember in each of these moments that you DO hear me. Help me lift my troubles up to you, my God. Instead of wallowing in the pain and turmoil, help me cry out to you. Thank you for hearing all of my prayers; all of the cries of my heart.

Thank you, Lord, for answering my prayers. Even if that answer does not come on the timeline that I think it should follow. Help me to submit my plans to you. I only want what you have planned for my life. Fill me with your grace and peace while I wait.

Thank you, Lord!

25

Hebrews 11:6

And it is impossible to please God without faith. Anyone who wants to come to him must believe that God exists and that he rewards those who sincerely seek him.

Lord,

I believe that you are all that you say you are. I believe that
you are the Creator of the world. I believe that you loved me
so much, that you gave your son to die as a sacrifice, in my
place. Nothing I could ever do, could earn what you have
freely given. Abba, I want to come to you. I long to be close
to you. Increase my vision and minister to my soul while I
wait. Help me to keep making the choice every day to serve
you. I know that you are good and faithful. As my Father, I
know you will reward me as I seek to devote my life to you.
All that I am is yours. Mold me into a pleasing sacrifice that
warms your heart. Bring me closer to you, closer than ever
before.

I earnestly seek you!

26

Psalm 18:6

But in my distress I cried out to the Lord; yes, I prayed to my God for help. He heard my cry from his sanctuary, my cry to him reached his ears.

Oh, Abba Daddy,

Thank you for being a real God. Thank you for loving us and meeting us in our distress. You know my heart. You feel my pain, you feel the weight my empty arms carry. Thank you for hearing me when I cry. Come now, wrap your arms around me, hold me, let me cry. Soothe my raw pain. Give me peace to get through this. Breathe in me. Renew my strength. Renew my hope. Help me to trust you, even when my circumstances only speak doubt. Be a balm to my soul. Comfort me, Holy Spirit. Help me to continue on this journey with a faith that does not fade amidst the pain. Wipe my tears, and love on me.

You are my good, good Father.

27

Psalm 89:33-35

But I will never stop loving him nor fail to keep my promise to him. No, I will not break my covenant. I will not take back a single word I said. I have sworn an oath to David, and in my holiness, I cannot lie.

Lord, I know you have clearly promised us a miracle, biological child. Thank you for being a holy God. Thank you that you are always good and always faithful. Thank you for loving me; even when I lose it and don't react as I should. Thank you for the encouraging reminder, that your Word is always true. You WILL keep your promise to me. I can trust you and have complete faith in you. Even when everything around me says to stop believing, I never will. You will not break your covenant, and you will not take back what you have said. Thank you for this promise of a child. Thank you for your love and faithfulness.

May my life bring you honor and glory, always.

28

Psalm 142:1-3

*I cry out to the Lord, I plead for the Lord's mercy.
I pour out my complaints before him and tell
him all my troubles. When I am overwhelmed,
you alone know the way I should turn.*

Abba Daddy,

My heart is full of sadness today. I so wanted today to be
a day of rejoicing, yet, I find that I cannot stop crying as
another month passes without a baby. Lord, I ask for your
mercy to be poured out on me. How long must my hope be
deferred? What must I do to see breakthrough in this? I am
feeling overwhelmed, and I am struggling to rally my heart to
believe again.

Thank you for being a God I can cry out to. Thank you
for letting me pour my heart out to you with no fear of
judgment. Thank you for your grace and mercy. They cover
me like a soft blanket that soothes my weeping. Guide me,
Lord. You alone know the way I should turn, what steps I
should take to move forward. Show me the way, Lord. Help
me to get up and walk in it.

Thank you for always being with me!

29

Psalm 143:7-8

Come quickly, Lord, and answer me, for my depression deepens. Don't turn away from me, or I will die. Let me hear of your unfailing love each morning, for I am trusting you. Show me where to walk, for I give myself to you.

Abba Daddy,

I cry out to you. I am tired of holding on. I am tired of struggling. I feel all the hurt. Every negative test, every deferred hope is weighing me down. I cannot continue to have faith and fully expect our miracle without your supernatural grace sustaining me. Flood me with your unfailing love, douse me in your compassion. Holy Spirit let me soak in your strength as you renew my hope. Help me to trust you without wavering. Show me where I should walk, guide me to follow your will for my life. My heart, my faith, my whole being is yours. Make me who you need me to be. Come to me quickly, Lord. You are my heart's desire.

I give myself to you, Lord.

30

Psalm 138:2-3

I bow before your holy Temple as I worship. I praise your name for your unfailing love and faithfulness; for your promises are backed by all the honor of your name. As soon as I pray you answer me; you encourage me by giving me strength.

Oh Lord, you are so much better to me than I deserve. I am humbled and stand in awe at the depth of your love for me. You never fail. You never lie. You always do what you have said you will do. Help me to worship you in love and honor. Help me to remember that a delay does not mean that you have forgotten your promises to me. Thank you for immediately hearing my prayers and answering me; even if that answer is to wait awhile longer.

Please encourage me. Give me the strength to persevere on this journey. Do not let my hope fade. Increase my faith and my thankfulness in who you are.

You are so good to me, always!

31

Romans 15:13

I pray that God, the source of hope, will fill you completely with joy and peace because you trust in him. Then you will overflow with confident hope through the power of the Holy Spirit.

Lord,

I am so thankful that you are my source of hope. I don't have to work so hard to stay cheerful. I don't have to strive to bury my hurt so no one knows. I appreciate that I can be real with you. You can handle my heart, my frustration, my despair. You take them all away. You lovingly wipe my tears and wrap me in your embrace.

Fill me completely with your joy and peace. Remind me that you are all-powerful. Nothing is too big for you. No diagnosis can prevent you from faithfully creating your miracle. Help me to rest in this. Help me to be a vessel that overflows with the confident hope your Holy Spirit gives. Show me someone today who is also hurting. Give me a boldness to approach them with gentle kindness, to share your hope, and to be a blessing to others.

Let your love pour out of me!

32

Jeremiah 29:11

For I know the plans I have for you, declares
the Lord. Plans to prosper, not to harm you.
Plans to give you hope and a future.

Precious Lord,

I just want to come before you and thank you. Thank you for being a big God. Thank you for being bigger than my fear. Thank you for reminding me that nothing takes you by surprise. A negative test is not a wrench in your plans, throwing you for a loop. You already know our future, you already have a plan to bring us good not harm, all the days of our life.

Thank you for the faith we can have in you. We trust that you are good. We know that you are faithful. Increase our trust and our faith as we wait for you to bring our great blessing to us. Thank you for loving us – despite our weakness and constant failures. Thank you for your grace and mercy. Thank you for longing to have a relationship with us. Holy Spirit, we invite you into our lives. Keep our hearts open to you. Fill us with your peace that passes all understanding.

Thank you, Lord!